TRADE UNION AND COLLECTIVE BARGAINING

ATHUL RAMASWAMI J S

Made with ♥ on the Notion Press Platform
www.notionpress.com

Contents

Preface

"Start writing, no matter what. The water does not flow until the faucet is turned on".

- Louis L'Amour

Hundreds of students and professors are contributing their work to Brain Booster Articles, we are here to provide ample information about Law and Contemporary issues. Our aim is to provide a platform for today's generation to express their views and ideas on law and contemporary law.

CHAPTER ONE

Abstract

The process by which workers or labourers negotiate the terms of their contracts with their employers is referred to as collective bargaining. During collective bargaining, employees and employers work together to resolve labour disputes amicably through negotiations and agreements. Because of India's slow industrialization, true collective bargaining became popular only after independence. Meanwhile, Indian laws recognised collective bargaining, including the levels and stages of the effective process. Finally, this makes negotiating with employers easier and more effective, and it aids in resolving issues without the use of courts or tribunals.

CHAPTER TWO

Introduction and History

Collective bargaining refers to the process by which workers or labourers negotiate the terms of their contracts with their employers. Laborers are typically represented by a trade or labour union. This is usually done in order to achieve certain labour demands and rights, such as working hours, wages, working conditions, and so on. This method of resolving industrial disputes has been revolutionary for labour relations in Indian industries, both private and public. This is because commercial and business conflicts are unavoidable, and it is impractical to resolve all such disputes through the courts. As a result, collective bargaining has emerged as a viable option for resolving industrial disputes.

In the course of collective bargaining, a company's employees and employer come together to amicably resolve labour conflicts through negotiations and agreements. Every employee has a right to engage in collective bargaining. In addition to engaging in concerted economic activity conflict resolution processes, it also entails employee unionisation, negotiations, administration, and interpretation of collective bargaining agreements affecting compensation, hours of work, other working conditions.

Only the employee and the employer are party to this bipartite process. The only parties with the authority to participate in the negotiation process are these two. The conversation is conducted collaboratively without the involvement of a third party.

Negotiations about working conditions and terms of employment between an employer, a group of employees, or one or more employers' organisations on the other, with a view to achieving an agreement, according to the International Labour Organization Manual from 1960.

Due to India's tardy industrialization, true collective bargaining only became popular after independence. Before India gained its independence, the first collective bargaining took place in an Ahmedabad textile mill when the workers there realised that going to court to resolve labour problems was a complete waste of time, effort, and resources in British-ruled India.

Following independence, the Indian Aluminium Company and Dunlop Rubber Company in West Bengal entered into the first collective agreement, which lasted for five years. Following this, several businesses began to use the notion of collective bargaining.

CHAPTER THREE

Definition

According to Article 2 of the Collective Bargaining Convention, 1981[1]of the International LabourOrganisation, "collective bargaining extends to all negotiations which take place between an employer, a group of employers or one or more employers' organisations, on the one hand, and one or more workers' organisations, on the other, for

(a) determining working conditions and terms of employment; and/or

(b) regulating relations between employers and workers; and/or

(c) regulating relations between employers or their organisations and workers or workers' organisations".

In the case of *Ram Prasad Viswakarma v. Industrial Tribunal[2]*, Prior to the introduction of collective bargaining, labourers found it extremely difficult to negotiate the terms and conditions of their contracts. Then, Collective bargaining became the norm with the advent of trade unions. It became more convenient for employers because they only had to negotiate with labour representatives rather than with each individual labourer.

In the case of *Bharat Iron Works v. BhagubhaiBalubhai Patel*,[3] It was discovered that collective bargaining is a component of the modern welfare state concept. It must be carried out in a healthy manner, with mutual cooperation between employers and employees. Negotiation between management and the trade union aids in the resolution of various issues.

[1]154)

[2] AIR 1961 SC 857

[3]AIR 1976 SC 98

CHAPTER FOUR

Indian legislation and court rulings recognising collective bargaining

1. Industrial Disputes Act, 1947

For the purpose of regulating the investigation and resolution of labour disputes, this Act was passed. According to Section 18 of the Act, any settlement reached by an agreement by an employer and his employees, other than a conciliation, shall be binding upon them. This basically means that Section 18 acknowledges the resolution of industrial disputes through collective bargaining.

2. Trade Union Act, 1926

This Act covers a trade union's registration, rights, obligations, and privileges. The most crucial role of a trade union is to control how a company or management interacts with its workforce.

In the 1952 case of *D.N. Banerjee v. P.R. Mukherjee*[1], it was noted that because labour and capital have grown more important in today's society, they have organised into groups to resolve disagreements. This is predicated on the idea that cooperation strengthens us, and that's how collective bargaining came about.

3. The Constitution of India, 1950

The fundamental rights and Directive principles of state policy are just two of the many articles included in the Indian Constitution that support the idea of collective bargaining. The right to form an association, which includes the right to form a trade union, is guaranteed under Article 19 of the Indian Constitution. The state is given the authority to enact laws under Article 43 A that promote employee participation in management.

4.   The Industrial Employment (Standing Orders) Act, 1946

Section 2(g) of this Act defines "standing order" as the procedures governing things like worker classification, attendance, leave eligibility requirements, how to inform employees of information about their jobs and pay, etc. According to Section 3 of the Act, the employer must first provide the Certifying Officer with a draft of the standing order and, to the greatest extent feasible, must follow the model established for the standing order. The Officer then sends copies of the document to the workers' union or to the unionised workers. The officer must give both parties a chance to be heard if there is no trade union to ask for objections before certifying the standing order with the necessary changes and sending copies to each party. Here, it is clear that the certifying officer serves as the mediator and that both the employer and the employees are involved in the process of crafting a standing order. In essence, this clause uses the collective bargaining process.

In *Hindustan Lever Ltd. Vs. Hindustan Lever Employees Union[2]*, where the Court has reaffirmed in a number of subsequent cases, acknowledges the importance of collective bargaining between workers and employers in modern economic life. Prior to the advent of collective bargaining, labour faced significant difficulties in obtaining appropriate service contract terms from his employer. Employers found it necessary and convenient to deal with workers' representatives rather than individual workers, not only when making or amending contracts, but also when taking disciplinary action against one or more workers, and in all other disputes, as the country's trade unions grew and collective bargaining became the norm.

Mrf United Workers Union Vs. Tamil Nadu State, 2009[3]

To determine whether an organisation is competent to be the sole signatory to collective agreements, two criteria should be used: representativeness and independence. The decision on whether organisations meet these requirements should be made by a body that ensures objectivity and independence.

As a result, it was argued on their behalf that it was an international standard for the trade union acting as the sole collective bargaining agent to be representative and independent.

P. Virudhachalam and others Vs. Lotus Mills' Administration[4]

It is important to remember that the Act is based on the concept of collective bargaining in order to settle industrial disputes and maintain industrial peace. In all collective bargaining negotiations, individual workers must inevitably fade into the background. The union that represents such employees takes over negotiating on his behalf. Unions advocate for a common cause on behalf of all of their members.

As a result, any agreement they reach with management binds at least their members and, if reached through conciliation processes, even non-members. As a result, settlements serve as the Act.

OBJECTIVES OF COLLECTIVE BARGAINING

- to encourage an amicable and pleasant working relationship between employers and employees.
- equal protection of the interests of the employer and the employees.
- to guarantee a minimal level of governmental intervention.
- to support the upkeep of a democratic workplace culture.

STAGES OF COLLECTIVE BARGAINING

1. FORMING A UNION- Seven employees are required to form a trade union, according to Section 9A of the Trade Unions Act of 1926. Although registering a union is not required, there are several benefits, including proper worker representation, the ability to use funds for specific goals, protection from legal lawsuits, etc.
2. MAKING A CHARTER OF DEMANDS: Either the union or the employer may start the collective bargaining process at this point. After multiple talks among all of its members, the labour union produces a charter of demands.
3. NEGOTIATION: The charter of demands is submitted to start the negotiations. In most cases, the union is the one who formally proposes modifications to the current collective bargaining agreements during the first meeting. The management is then given the chance to make counterproposals. They keep doing this until they reach a consensus. A third person may be chosen as a mediator or arbitrator if they are unable

to come to an agreement on their own.

4. <u>STRIKES:</u> The union has the right to call a strike if negotiations are unsuccessful. Employees in the public utility industry are required to give six weeks' notice of a strike under Section 22 of the Industrial Disputes Act, and they have fourteen days to strike after giving that notice. While the conciliation is ongoing and for seven days following the conclusion of the conciliation processes or for two months following the conclusion of the legal proceedings, neither management nor the union may engage in any form of industrial action.

5. <u>FORMING AN AGREEMENT:</u> The procedure starts when the conciliation officer receives a notice of strike. You have two alternatives to pick from in this stage. According to Section 4 of the Act, the state government may appoint a conciliation officer to look into, mediate, and encourage settlement during the cooling-off period. The second choice is for the state government to establish a Board of Conciliation, which would have a chairperson and two or four members, in accordance with Section 5 of the Act. Strikes are prohibited throughout the conciliation process, in accordance with Sections 22 and 23 of the Act. According to Section 20 of the Act, this process ends with a settlement or a reference to an industrial tribunal or labour court.

6. <u>ARBITRATION:</u> If the conciliation procedure fails, the parties may choose to arbitrate either voluntarily or involuntarily, and the arbitrator's recommendations may have legal force. A state's labour court or industrial tribunal may decide certain disputes, according to Section 7A of the Act. In order to settle disputes involving matters of national importance, national tribunals may be established under Section 7B of the Act. The case may be sent by written agreement between the employer and the employees to a national tribunal, industrial tribunal, or labour court for arbitration or adjudication.

[1]AIR 1953 SC 58
[2] 1994 SUPPL. (4) SCR 723
[3]2010 LLR 165
[4]1998 (1) SCT 262

CHAPTER FIVE

Different levels of collective bargaining

Whether it is a craft level conflict or a national level dispute, disputes occur at every level in a corporation. the differences in collective bargaining standards between regions, unions, etc. It is simpler to handle the issue and forecast how the industry will behave when an organisation classifies its labour disputes according to levels.

Union to union, industry to industry, and region to area, there are different levels of collective bargaining. This simultaneously makes the study of collective bargaining more challenging and fascinating. Collective bargaining at various levels reflects the cultures, ideas, and attitudes of both the management and the unions.

1. NATIONAL - LEVEL BARGAINING

The national union and the employer's organisation typically engage in collective bargaining at the national level. Representatives from both parties meet to negotiate on crucial and fundamental topics. Negotiation topics at the national level can include pay, direct benefits, or shift benefits. All industries and all industrial workers accept issues when national bargaining takes place. The homogeneity and standardisation of pay and wage structures are benefits of negotiation at this level. Conflict and inequity are avoided. When the workforce is small and homogenous, this degree of negotiation is widely accepted. The issue with this sort of negotiating is that it is impossible in India due to the size of the nation and the uneven distribution of the labour force.

2. INDUSTRY LEVEL BARGAINING

When collective bargaining occurs at the industry level, employers from one industry bargain with unions from that industry. These unions are organised in the form of industry federations. Basic wages, allowances, production capacity, production norms, and working conditions in that industry are all negotiated and bargained for. Bargaining at the industry level ensures that labour costs and working conditions are consistent across industries.

3. CORPORATE LEVEL BARGAINING

Corporate collective bargaining occurs when the management of a company with many plants negotiates a single contract with different unions on behalf of all of its plants. Corporate management typically conducts the collective bargaining along with representatives from several plants. The benefit of corporate level bargaining is that it ensures consistency across all of its locations and prevents conflicts that result from imbalance.

4. PLANT LEVEL BARGAINING

The majority of Indian private sector businesses frequently engage in collective bargaining at the plant level. A factory establishment's or a specific plant's management engages in collective bargaining at the plant level. The problems solely affect that manufacturing or plant. Such agreements are based on performance-related or pay productivity-related issues. The independent nature of the negotiations is the second benefit of plant level bargaining.

CHAPTER SIX

Conclusion

Trade unions' historical function in India was largely confined to collective bargaining for financial reasons. Contrarily, trade unions today play a significant role in the welfare of employees, cultural initiatives, banking, and healthcare facilities, as well as in promoting awareness through the training and education of trade union members.

Due to heightened competition, however, the main managerial goals in collective bargaining in recent years have been to lower labour costs, boost output or productivity, increase work flexibility (multi-skilling/multifunctioning, changes in worker grades, etc.), lengthen workdays, cut regular staff strength via VRS, emphasise quality and so forth.

To sum up, the creation of a collective bargaining agreement is a crucial phase in the process of collective bargaining between the employer and the employees. Employers and unions turn to this as a last option for resolving conflicts. It is created as a result of an effective voluntary nature negotiation. This makes the process of negotiating with employers easier and more effective and assists in resolving issues without the assistance of courts or tribunals.